A Prelude to the

I have separated my choice into eight sections
to simplify navigating the book, the sections are:
'Family' - 'Hull' - 'Remembrance' - 'Time' - 'America' -
'Reflections' - 'Road Rage' - 'Haikus' .

ᎧᏃ

Some people say that writing poetry is only
done by romantic or idealistic fools and has no real place
in modern literature, others state that it is one of the hardest
and most difficult forms of writing that there is - two polar
opposites and in between is every shade of opinion imaginable,
which makes me either a romantic/idealistic old fool, or a
practitioner of one of the hardest and most difficult etc . . .
I'm a poet, or I like to think of myself as one.
Please read the poems and maybe, hopefully, you will
form your own opinion.

John Fairclough

1

This book is for my family and my friends,
without whose encouragement it would never have
seen the light of day.
My special thanks go to my wife Maureen
and my daughter Nicole, for all their help and
encouragement, to my friend
Phil Corby for his technical input, artistic wizardry
and honest opinions, to Monty and James
and all my friends at Barton Muse . . .
and to all the people who have ever applauded
when I have stood up and read my poems.
My thanks to you all.

Cover: Original Oil Painting by John Fairclough

The author asserts the moral right under the copyright, designs and patents act 1988 to be identified as the author of this work.
Copyright John Faiclough 2019

ISBN 978-1-9161028-0-4

Design and artwork by Phil Corby
Printed by Fisk Printers Hull

Contents

Contents

Family

"When mother was eighty, we gave her a party."

*This is the opening line of a poem called 'Family Reunion'
written by my eldest sister,
(see 'The Thread' by Doreen Tagholm)
the closing lines were as follows:-*

*"Proving again that whatever the heartaches,
Families breed something - could it be love?"*

*I hope that this next selection of poems will
go some way towards proving her point . . .*

Siblings

We stand in a group, the six of us,
with mother seated in front, and, as always,
looking over her shoulder and up to Do',
something which we all of us know
she did for most of her life -
an unconscious gesture - for assurance,
for comfort, an urging to forgive?
for something which I've always known
that I could never give.

With Margaret, as usual, telling someone
off camera just what to do,
and Mick close behind her, almost
hidden from view, almost an outsider,
except to me, for we were as close
as any brothers could be,
and Mary, soft smiling, with her eyes far away,
her expression remembering some other day.

And Audrey, always self conscious in front of the lens,
guarding the image which she always defends
with a somewhat fixed and wooden smile,
whilst the children, meanwhile, are just being children,
always changing places, laughing angelic faces,
taking no notice of the camera at all,
and hard as I try, I can never recall
just what it was that Do' and I were laughing at that day,
but there we stay, laughing forever?

Stepping to Life's Tune

She's the eldest, with a love of life
which is unshakeable,
a love so strong it can withstand
the horror headlines of today,
and yet so tender, in its way,
that words and music can bring her to tears.

She's the eldest, the one who, in a crisis,
the whole family turns to,
the one who will never ridicule,
or condemn, or in any way malign,
the one who always, time after time,
turns the other cheek.

She's the eldest, and by far the wisest,
and though I already know that I'm
somewhat biased, she's the one who
seems to me to have got the priorities
where they ought to be, with life itself
stepping to the tune she plays.

She's the eldest, always the one standing
next to me, with that closely shared affinity
which can catch my every mood or feeling,
even though we may be miles apart,
and I like to think, within my heart,
that though we may not always step
to the same drummer, we both of us hear
the same beat - however measured or faraway.

Two of my sisters, Doreen and Mary, and myself, all shared a love of poetry,
both reading it and writing it (see 'Postcards and poetry' page 18)
I sent the above poem to Do'.

Overleaf was her reply:-

For John

There are moments which flood the heart,
Blurring vision, choking sound-
A blend of pain and pleasure so exquisite
It seems it could never happen again;
But it does - oh, it does,
In a surge of Bruch or Mahler,
In the anticipated and unfailing hook
Of a Gershwin song, a passage of Updike,
Or the heartbreak blue of morning glory;
And only today, and as piercing sweet,
Another - A bonus, an extra, a poem,
For me, from my brother.

Doreen Tagholm

The Flag of Happiness

Herewith, and with love, it said on the card,
and there inside, written in her neat and flowing hand,
was a message which everyone could understand,
a seven line poem, short, soft, yet so pristine,
the sentiments clearly there to be seen -
touch the hand, meet the eye, say I love you,
and watch the sky fill up with wonder,
as the great flag of happiness unfurls.

With apologies to my big sister Doreen

Maybe Now

Maybe now you know,
maybe now you are beginning to understand,
to comprehend the feeling,
the awesome, overwhelming, often unbearable
mixture of hope, responsibility, joy, sorrow,
and pride, which is the love I have,
(and sometimes have to hide) for you, my only child.

Maybe now, as you watch your own children grow,
You will begin to know, to understand,
how I feel about you.
How I delight in the things which you do,
how all your life you have been that bright star,
constantly shining, lighting up my life with your laughter,
and sometimes, killing me softly with your tears,
with all the unknown fears I feel for your future.

Maybe now, as I am growing old,
and winter cold is creeping into my system,
maybe now you'll begin to understand
and know that we cannot stop old age,
although in Dylan's words I rage and rage,
against the dying of the light.
I know that I have only yesterday,
since you are grown and gone away,
but, maybe now, as your own children grow,
you'll begin to know, and to understand.

For Doreen

It was called 'The thread' and when I first read it
I was moved to tears by its content,
by the picture in my mind of my sister,
her dark head bent, working over her hooky mat,
her face a picture as she sat, listening,
waiting to hear his cry.

All poetry is a personal thing, and somehow
she had managed to bring in those few lines,
all the love and the care, all the feelings
which only mothers can bear for their children.
And reading, I somehow wished that I could make words
mean so much, could use them with so deft a touch
they could convey such depth of feeling.

Philosophy

"It's not a practice" my brother said
in his blunt and forthright way,
"You only get one go at life, so try
and live each day as if you mean it!"
and he grinned at me, pleased with
his homespun philosophy.

And I smiled at him and thought how true
his throwaway line could be,
for we all live our lives and fail to see
the writing on the wall,
and later so few of us can ever recall
the times when our lives changed.

So strange, that none can ever remember the day
when ambition seemed to drain away,
and we began to settle for what we had,
began to accept the good and the bad
which mark our march through life.

And now she's dying and I'm two hundred miles away,
regretting all the things I didn't say,
and never did, yet glad somehow
for all the memories made and saved,
just for those cold and rainy days
of bitter sweet regret.

And so I sit here, alone with my tears,
looking back over her crowded years,
and wondering if my philosopher brother
can explain to me just why, a grown man sits alone to cry,
on such a pleasant June evening.

Words

Inside the cover, on the flysheet it read,
"From Mam and Dad, with love, 1958."
And as I read the inscription again,
written in that old fashioned, trembling hand,
I wondered, did they ever understand
how much they had endeared themselves to me
by this gift, sponsored and chosen, I am sure,
by their daughter, now my wife,
but throughout my life I will forever treasure it,
and the memory of their understanding
and acceptance of me.

*'Words' is the title of a dictionary, given to me by my wife's parents
as a Christmas present in 1958. Today it is old, and much battered
and repaired through long usage - but it still has pride of place
on my bookshelves . . .*

Almost a Year

It's been almost a year now, and in silent awe
I wonder just how she manages to be so calm,
so clear, almost serene, I mean, had it been me
I would have raged, raged, against the injustice
of it all.

But she remains almost unchanged and it seems
so strange, being so close to her, to watch,
as with such gentle care, she puts our friends at ease,
almost as if she sees and senses their apprehension,
and fear of talking about it.

Oh I know there have been tears, from both of us,
tears from her, for things which now can never be the same,
and tears of fear, of a thing unknown for which there is no name,
and tears of rage, which I have shed, beating against the helpless
dread of that unknown fear, which always now seems to lay so near.

It's been almost a year now, and still I sit here,
wondering just how and where she finds the strength to care
and somehow always to be there, whenever she is most needed.
But in the silent reaches of the night, laying sleepless,
with her by my side, I'm thankful the darkness is there to hide my
tears, as silently I rage and rage against the injustice of it all.

Angels in the Roof Beams

They sit up on the roof beams,
their cherubic faces always smiling,
beguiling us into believing in them
as they watch over our daily lives.
And each Christmas day there's a new addition,
and a note which states, with some contrition,
"Someone to watch over you"-
and maybe they do, I cannot say,
but asked -"Do you really believe in them?"
I look across at her and think,
Just let them work for her, and I'll believe.

My Daughter

She is the lights on the Christmas tree,
she is the child on its mothers knee
she is the quiet of an empty church,
she is the place I know my search
for happiness will always end.

She is the prayer answered in the night,
she is the birthday child's delight,
she is the sunlight through a stained glass window,
she is the one who I always know
will play life's game with total honesty.

She is the snowdrops in the spring,
she is the feeling a song can bring,
she is the sound of children's laughter,
she is the happy ever after,
for she is the child with her mother's eyes,
the child whose smile forever lies
within her father's heart.

She is all these things, and more,
a fund of memories which I store
and keep for that cold and rainy day,
when she is grown and gone away,
for she was the child with her mother's eyes,
the child whose smile forever lies
within her father's heart.

Bookman

My father was a clever man, not academic, but who can be
when they only get a primary education.
No, he had more a sort of odd job intelligence,
picked up from books mostly, for he was deaf,
and the written word meant more to him,
and though my memory now is dim,
I can still recall his books.
He'd read most anything he could, religion, travel,
fact or fiction, they all served his long addiction
for the written word.

My father was a clever man, and maybe
it was a deliberate plan, to catch my interest,
I don't know, but always books were there,
left open in the soft armchair for me to find,
and read and read, and I'm sure he knew the magic seed
that with each book he planted.
He died a long, long time ago, but I would love to let him know,
How well his plan succeeded.

Published in 'Proof' magazine May, 1985.

Days of Miracle and Wonder

I watch them growing day by day,
sometimes afraid to turn away
for fear of missing some slight change,
a different tilting of the head, a new word said,
the first game fully understood,
the feeling that somehow I should
be re-arranging my life to share their being.

Tight circle of their whole hand around my finger,
that feeling which I know will linger
all my life, a circle of bright light around the bone,
the sweetest touch I've ever known.
The undisguised joy of their noisy greeting,
as if our every morning meeting was the first,
as with outstretched arms they leap to my embrace,
each laughing face fighting for my attention.

And as I watch them growing, day by day,
I know that too soon they'll be walking away,
and these so few days will be gone and lost,
and my heart aches counting the coming cost,
as I hold on to these days of miracle and wonder.

Postcards and Poetry

For so many years it was almost a ritual, the postcards and the poetry.
They flitted between Do' and Mary, and me, like so many snowflakes.
Postcards from where we had been, and what we had seen, and done,
covering every topic under the sun, from family affairs to world affairs.

Art, Books, Exhibitions, - villages, cities, museums,
Wherever we went and whatever we did - there would be a postcard.

The poetry was almost always our own (with notable exceptions)
From Do' heartfelt, witty, often caustic - yet written with such sparse
and gentle elegance.

Whilst from Mary's poems always a sense of neat and tidy orderliness
as befitted a schoolteacher.

And me, I wrote, (and am still writing) reams and reams of very
common verse .

Mary and I still write, and phone each weekend -
and life goes on, but, with Do' now gone, we both know it can
never be the same, and like a game, played long ago by children,
the halcyon days of postcards and poetry are over and only bitter
sweet memories remain.

♔ HULL

The truth will be known . . . Is the title
of the poem which is inscribed around the base of an installation
in Hull city centre, in the form of a sphere, approx. nine feet
in diameter it has on its surface inscribed all the
names of the streets, roads, avenues, etc. which
were bombed during the blitz of the city
during WW2.

Under each name there is a further
list of the names of all the people
in that street who were killed by
the bombs - the names run into
thousands.

The poem inscribed beneath and
printed on the following page
goes some way to explaining the
attitude of the people of Hull -
they are strong-willed, fiercely
independent, highly suspicious
of any form of authority and
totally loyal to their home town.

My hope is that the poems in this
section will reflect this . . .

One day at last the truth will be known.
And all the world shown forth.

That the worst...
was that town so...

19

The truth will be known

On The North East Coast of England,
By a river long and wide,
Stands a wrecked and broken city,
Smashed by a Nazi tide.
The Luftwaffe came in increasing wave,
Destruction and death in its wake.
But the townsfolk, sturdy, strong and brave,
Showed them just how much they could take.
A town on the North East Coast has been bombed,
Some Casualties few believed dead.
London and Coventry bombed again,
Was the news that was usually read.

One day at last the truth will be known,
And all the world shown forth.
That the worst bombed place in England,
Was that town in the north.
Yes, the bricks of the city were razed to the ground,
Not a single street was left full,
But the soul of the people was raised to the skies,
The soul of the people of Hull.

Clarry Hovell

Living on the Edge

It's not a city you would pass through
On your way to somewhere else,
Oh no, if you arrive here
Then this is where you want to be,
for beyond here are only fields,
and the ever present sea,
stretching out to the far horizon.
Here there is only north, east and west,
There is no south at all
Unless you want to count the river,
Which is, in fact, an estuary,
But is aways referred to, locally,
As simply, 'the Humber'.
Here you can walk past stores
Which have a sign outside their doors
Reading 'Welcome' in Swedish,
Danish, Dutch, and German,
A city which has more in common
With Amsterdam than with London,
A city set against the water's edge
As if to pledge its loyalty
To the restless, ever present sea,
a city of seagulls, wheeling and climbing
against the north winds unrelenting surge,
then diving to pick, and peck, and purge.
A northern city of blues and greys,
Out on its own, living its days
In splendid isolation, Oh no,
If you arrive here, then this is where
You want to be, and that, for me,
Is just the way I want it.

City Without a Cathedral

I grew up here, in this city, city without a cathedral,
on a council estate known as 'Corn Beef Island'-
a name which then I didn't understand,
and which even now I'm not too sure about,
- though the story goes that corned beef was all
that the council tenant could afford to eat,
and like most northern humour, seems somehow neat,
and sharply to the point!

I grew up here, in this city where, if the wind's direction
wasn't quite right, there was the smell
of the fish docks all day and all night.
A three sided city, living on the edge of the Humber,
And to a boy then as young as me,
A place of excitement and mystery,
Watching the fleet ride the evening tide,
As they started out on that long cold ride,
To the far northern fishing grounds.

I grew up here, in this city, in long flat streets
where the bicycle was king, where the biting wind
would always bring my father home, his gaunt face lined,
from work which was always hard to find, from the docks,
the sidings, and in his docker's slang, from the
bloody white slavery of the deal carrying gang.

Yes, I grew up here, in this city without a cathedral,
Grew up with its isolation, with its almost cultivated
northern harshness, speaking its hard edged accent,
and knowing full well just what was meant
when people spoke of hardship.
 And yet stubbornly proud of being a part of it,
Of living here, out on the edge,
Feeling somehow I should always pledge
My continuing loyalty to its unrelenting independence.

The Fishing Fleet

It stands on the edge of a wide expanse
of estuary, where the tides advance
up, over the mud flats, brown and slippy,
and on down the river that halves this city,
the river that is both friend and foe,
for it brings in wealth, but it brings in woe,
for in days gone by, when the spring tides came,
many low lying homes were never the same
when the flood tide ebbed.

But now a great barrier can be dropped into place,
which stops forever the flood tide's race,
if only a barrier that like could have dropped,
something that would forever have stopped
the fishing fleet draining away.
But they're all gone now, those once proud ships,
which carried the men on those long cold trips
to the far northern fishing grounds.
They're gone, and soon few will remember the days
when St Andrew's dock was a cobweb maze
of nets and tackle, sheet and rope,
a place of vigour, work and hope.
Now once proud ships stand empty and bare,
and the smell of decay is hovering there,
and rusting plates are reminders grim
of the penalties of the market's whim.

And the Hessle Road streets are strangely sad,
for gone is the laughter they once had,
gone is the laughter, the brawls and the fights,
the blow all your wages Saturday nights,
when the trawlers all came home.
And somehow the feeling just isn't the same,
though it's nothing to which you could put a name,
just something that's gone which can never return,
an era, an age, a sense of pace,
something that time could never replace,
it's just some evenings when I'm standing there,
and the memories seem to fill the air,
I recall, with such a bitter pride,
when the fishing fleet rode the evening tide,
to the far northern fishing grounds.

Published in 'Proof' Magazine, May 1984.

Land of Northern Light

And now I must return to my land
of northern light,
to the names that ring familiar
in my mind,
to watch again the seagulls swooping down
round Sammy's Point,
to walk down Mytongate and know I'll find
King Billy, still astride his horse,
his gold reflection glistening
from pavements wet with morning rain,
to walk down High Street once again
and see the old 'Black Boy'.

For now I must return to my land
of northern light,
to the accent that falls easy on my ear,
to hear again the slapping of the paddles
on the ferry as it sidles up to Corporation Pier.
To listen to the people with their hard
flat northern voices as they bargain hunt
around the market hall,
and to savour just the flavour of the chips
all wrapped in paper that you get
from old Bob Carver's chippy stall.

For now I must return to my land
of northern light,
to the places that are like old friends to me,
to watch the river winding
through the city, under bridges,
on its way out to the gleaming estuary.
And to smile with secret pleasure when the people
from outside us cannot ever find or understand
our quaint and fabled 'land of green ginger'.

Hull's Poet

And now there can be no more High Windows,
no more Whitsun Weddings,
no more lines that cut like knives,
or warm like glowing fire
with words that not so much inspire,
(although they do), but seem to hold me captive,
as if in awe, of someone with so fine a sense of time.

To think he lived but half an hour's walk from here,
to be so near, and yet so far away,
a fellow citizen, living and working in my home town,
a poet of such wide renown, he could have been the laureate,
but now he's gone, passed on, down the long slide to happiness,
and there inside the local press, half way down the page it read,
"Hull's poet, Philip Larkin-Dead."

Published in ' A lasting calm' the international library of poetry, 1997.

Larkin'about

Suddenly the city was filled with toads,
a metre high, and brightly painted fibreglass,
they were everywhere, in parks, and squares,
and shopping centres, it seemed that
every place you entered, there was a
psychedelic amphibian.

"They don't do poetry, they do rugby league"
It was said, "They'll all be vandalised"
but instead they were idolised, sponsored,
adopted, - people met by the tiger's toad,
and children were photographed
astride the pink spotted one.

The local Waterstones ran out of copies
of 'High Windows', and no-one knows
how many people followed the Toad Trail,
but sixty thousand maps of it were snapped up
within a week, and the university had to seek
a special licence for a night of his beloved jazz.

This is a city that is in the world, yet sufficiently
on the edge of it to have a different resonance,
and, in his precisely descriptive words, 'a sudden elegance'
he liked the simple clarity and no-nonsense attitude,
though often he was quite rude about everything that is here,
yet now his Pearson Park flat has become a poet's pilgrimage.

Now, like Betjeman in St. Pancras, he has his own statue
in Paragon Station, and though many in this nation
may view it with dismay, and would not recognize the line
'I was late getting away' the people in this city know it well,
for they are all poets,- and they can tell good writing
when they see it, - and good rugby league.

Chrome Curly 'echin

Chrome plated it was,
from the exotically shaped front forks
to the rear wheel sprocket,
it was a truly legendary racing rocket,
with Benelux gears and double clanger*
it simply oozed with potent glamour,
a true precision racing machine,
the first that our club had ever seen.

And that Saturday, at the first club 'ten' of the season,
I saw it again, and without reason
jealousy flared as it flashed away,
sending a silver dancing spray of sunlight
from its whirling wheels,
leaving me wondering just how it feels
to race on such a machine.

But I saw the race times at the end of the day,
and my jealousy quickly faded away,
for it hadn't lived up to its visual promise,
and with a time of only 34.24
I knew its rider would have to do much more
than just sit there and polish the lovely chrome,
if he wanted to beat some of our lads home.
And I smiled, tired, as I rode away,
pleased to have beaten evens that day,
and thinking quietly to myself,
"it's much too flashy anyway."

*In 1954 I was a member of the 'Hull Thursday Cycling Club' and would
take part in all the 10mile and 25mile time trials, and the weekend rides
up to Bridlington, Scarborough, and Whitby.*

** A 'double clanger' is a front chain wheel with two changeable teeth ratios
which doubles the number of ratios available from the back Benelux gears.
Old technology now, but state of the art back then.*

Saturday Ritual

All Saturday morning you'd watch out for the weather,
and hope, as you gathered your gear together,
that the rain would not be much, it was bad enough
being cold and tired, without being muddy wet, and yet,
you knew that even if the rain came down in buckets,
you'd still go, for part of the creed was always to show
that you were prepared to play.

In the old wooden changing rooms, with all your mates there,
and the jokes and the banter as you all prepare,
the Vaseline smeared over eyebrows and nose,
and that queasy sick feeling which never quite goes
until the match begins.
The rubbing oil smell, and the clammy cold strips,
and the team sheet called out with the coach's last tips,
then the boots to be checked at the side of the pitch,
and the captains instructions, "We'll try doing a switch
the first chance we get!"

Then high in the air the kick-off is curled,
and you take it and run, with no thought in the world
of the danger, and all through the match,
through its tackles and tries you hear
hard northern accents shouting the cries,
and like tribal chants they ring in your ears
until pain is forgotten and you have no fears,
"Come on forwards, back up!" and "Use the short ball"
and the winger breaks left, there's no cover at all,
and you follow him shouting, "Take out, I've got in"
and you tackle the centre knowing this one you'll win.

Then back in the changing hut, with a bottle of beer,
you slump back, eyes closed, wondering "Why am I here?"
getting battered and bruised, and feeling the pain,
yet knowing next week you'll be back here again,
is it to show that you're still a hard man,
or is it simply to show them that you still can!
and you hand in your strip, and you gather your gear,
and you think to yourself, "Well, maybe next year,
I'll give it all up!". . . ."well, maybe". . . .

Northern City

I walked around all the installations,
already knowing the stories they were telling,
my heart swelling with pride as I saw
the colourful displays on the city's buildings,
this city where I had spent most of my life,
where I had lived through the strikes and the strife,
the bombed building playgrounds of my childhood years,
all the uncertainty, and all the fears, and the isolation,
the derision, of being that 'northern city' whose name no-one knew.
And yet all my life that fierce pride of being a part of it,
of sharing that hard edged accent, of knowing full well
just what people meant when they spoke of hardship.
And now, suddenly, here it is, displayed for all the world to see,
This untold story of my city, - and of me!
I walked amongst the people of Hull on that night,
filled with pride at the sound and the sight,
of what we have achieved,
knowing that our unknown 'northern city' had finally
gained its long overdue recognition, its coming of age.
and my heart raced as I gazed all around,
filled with the sight and the wonderful sound,
of a city proud of its history, its heritage,
and its rightful sense of place.

The Legend of Dead Bod

It was on a dark and stormy night. . .

There were three Hull fishermen all at sea,
Two said to the other . . ."Tell us a story"

So he began . . .

"It was on a dark and stormy night" . . .

"There were three poets all at sea,
Monty, Big Phil, and me."
They said "Read us a poem."

So I began . . .

"It was on a dark and stormy night . . .
There came a gull in sightless flight
It hit the deck, and broke its neck,
And lay there dead, poor sod."

The End. (Inspired by a bit of silliness written by Phil Corby)

*And thus began the legend of Hull's
infamous 'Dead Bod'*

*'Dead Bod' is a piece of graffiti drawn
(very large) by a trawlerman on the corrugated
iron door of a quayside building on Albert dock,
Hull.
It depicts a white outline painting of a bird,
laid on its back with its feet in air, and the
legend 'Dead Bod' underneath. It became a
landmark for returning trawlermen, and has
recently been moved and installed as a piece of
ironic artwork in a Humber street gallery.*

REMEMBRANCE

'Remembrance' can be a very difficult subject to write about, for it can have so many different meanings and implications. It can be both sad or happy, personal or universal, unique to one person or shared by many - we all have our own interpretation of it.

These next poems are my remembrances. They are both personal (The camp) and more universal (A cry for peace).

Remembrance Recall
Recollection-Memory
Retrospect-Reminisce
Unforgettable-Memory
Reflect-Reminder
Remember-Reflect
Memories-Recall
emembrance

A Cry for Peace

I watch its progress through the town,
past the silent crowd, the legions lowered flags,
the futile gesture of flowers on the hearse,
and worse, the bewildered faces of the very young
as they stare, uncomprehending.
Sometimes it is only one, sometimes two, often more,
as with unthinking cynicism they keep a running score,
almost as if it were an international competition,
for with macabre repetition, they catalogue the dead,
each life a family laid to waste
Which leaves me such a bitter taste,
for I cannot reconcile the reason with the outcome,
and though maybe it's only me who's playing dumb,
but exactly what is it that we are trying to do,
to conquer them, subdue them, to turn them to our point of view?
Many armies have tried, and only their countless dead remain,
and the hills run red with rusting armour, and blood,
as with hooded eyes the Afghans stare,
their faces blank as they prepare another IED*
and silently seek the death of all infidels
And I wonder why our leaders still insist that it goes on,
our good intentions now all gone, lost in the dust of a futile war,
yet still we keep this endless score, and honour those lost in battle,
and as the eulogies are yet again read, the soft silence is broken
by the bewildered crying of the very young.

*IED Improvised Explosive Device

Entitlement

I watched them marching past today,
lined faces, spectacles, hair turned grey,
the turnout smaller than a year ago,
and in your heart you already know
that soon all the originals will have gone,
and you wonder then, how much longer
will they carry on?.

There were those in the ranks about my age,
some younger, men who were in the Gulf,
or the Falklands, or Cyprus, or even Korea,
who faced up to death, who must have known fear,
their medals sparse against the rows worn
by the older men, but then, I thought,
just as bravely earned, and worn now
with that same quiet pride.

"You could have marched," she said, breaking into
my thoughts. "You were in the army, you're entitled to."
And I looked at her, and saw her brother, Tom,
killed only weeks after landing in France,
and I turned quickly away, so that she had no chance
to see my expression, or the tears that clouded my eyes.
"Entitled," I thought, looking again at the rows
of glinting medals, and in my mind's eye seeing again
the neat and tidy rows of headstones and crosses.
"Entitled maybe-but not earned".

T.R. Metheringham. Killed in action 16th July 1944

Requiem for Tom

You will never know her as I do Tom,
for you were the older brother, who went off to war,
the brother who, when she was just four,
bought her a dress which didn't fit,
a present from a big brother who was going away,
with your mother angry at you all day
for wasting the clothing coupons.

You will never know how bewildered and lost
she was when the telegram came,
for to her it seemed to be almost a game,
a wonderment of watching her mother cry,
for she was too young to question why?
as the family all gathered on that sombre day.

You will never know how often she cried,
at the eleventh hour of the eleventh day,
as the bugle notes faded softly away,
and the poppies would fall, and prayers would be said,
and the poem to the fallen was once again read.

But I could feel your presence on that sunny day,
when we came, from so many miles away,
after fifty four years, with her family all gone,
and her the only remaining one,
she came to find you, to honour your grave,
to mark the sacrifice that you made,
her tears more eloquent than all the flowers
laid on the silent stones which filled
that warm and pleasant meadow in Normandy.

A Space for Tom

As I walk the hill there is soft silence everywhere,
the leafless trees are hazy shapes in the lingering mist,
as seagulls on motionless wings glide by,
grey shapes upon a grey and shrouded sky,
and I, walking alone - with only my thoughts for company.

It is twelve forty-five on Remembrance Sunday,
and I have left the village cenotaph at the foot of the hill,
left the old soldiers who are gathered there still,
left the swopping of stories of battles so bold,
and the memories of comrades who will never grow old.

I walk through the mist with my thoughts far away,
remembering the warmth of that sun dappled day
in Normandy, as we stood in that small meadow,
and you reached out, your hand resting on the warm stone,
as you wept for the brother you had no chance to have known.

Killed in action, I think the telegram read,
but you were too young to understand he was dead,
and you were much to young then to even know how to grieve,
or to even perceive the true weight of your loss,
only now, so many years later, there is a small
empty space in your heart which is forever marked . . . Tom.

And as I walk the hill there is a soft silence everywhere.

Flanders Fields

"Flanders fields" the headline read,
and at first glance, it must be said,
I thought it was just a list, a list of
the fallen, a roll of honour,
etched on a cenotaph erected in
some far off field in Flanders,
and I was briefly touched by nationalistic pride,
something we English will always hide,
as if somehow ashamed of our soldiers bravery.

But then, glancing down the alphabetically
listed inscriptions, at the regimental descriptions,
there on the list of the fallen, it suddenly stood out,
and like an unheard scream, a silent shout,
I found myself staring at my own name,
and suddenly I felt the tug of history, of family,
of someone, totally unknown to me,
but bearing my name, who had died
in those far off Flanders fields.

And for a moment I caught a glimpse,
a fleeting, tiny insight into the past,
a memory of times now elapsed, a name
carved out of stone, a token of a life
unknown to me, but one which will forever be
etched within my mind's eye, as the bugles notes die,
and the poem to the fallen is read,
in the silent stillness of the eleventh hour.

Heroes

There were no medals, no big parades,
no ticker tape welcomes, no motorcades,
there were no bands by the railroad track,
and no-one came out to welcome them back.
Only military bases, heartless and bare,
with only their families allowed to be there,
with only their fathers to weep for their sons,
with only their mothers to see what guns
and war could do to their children.

Some walked to their families, their gaunt eyes red,
some hobbled on crutches as tears were shed,
there were those who could neither hobble or walk,
there were those who never again would talk,
there were those whom the horror of what they'd been through
would taint forever the world which they knew,
there were those who said nothing, their minds all gone,
their sanity shattered by what they had done.

They came from the aircraft in a staggering line,
with the crippled and wounded ones leading the blind,
they had fought for their country in an undeclared war,
and lost, and were home to face up to the score,
of losing a war which they never could win,
which to America is the worst kind of sin.

So there were no medals, no big parades,
no ticker tape welcome, no motorcades,
there were no bands by the railroad track,
and no-one came out to welcome them back,
there was only a silence as cold as the tomb,
for the Vietnam veterans who made it back home.

Homecoming

Don't talk to me of heroes bright,
for today I witnessed a tragic sight,
when a piper played a lone lament,
and the generals stood, their bare heads bent,
on a rain swept dockside, cold and grey,
and I heard again the echoes
which marked that mournful day.

For I remember my fear on that fateful day
when I watched the ships as they slipped away,
with all the brave young faces, the waving hands,
the fluttering flags and marching bands,
that soon I would see them come home again,
their cold still bodies beyond all pain.
And I felt such sorrow at the price we pay,
as I heard again the echoes which marked that mournful day.

So don't talk to me of heroes bright,
of the victory march which looked so right,
don't boast to me how we won the war,
for today I witnessed the final score.
For it matters not who won or lost,
For nothing can counter the final cost,
and I weep as I think of the lives thrown away,
as I hear again the echoes which mark this mournful day.

Allahu Akbar

He came like a ghost through the dust ladened air
of that beleagued city,
his arms held aloft as they carried there
that tiny bundle of pity,
"Allahu Akbar" they cried, as he stood there
amid all the carnage and slaughter,
"Allahu Akbar" he softly echoed
as gently he lowered his daughter.

But I saw the grief in his hollow eyes,
and I heard the break in his voice,
and I knew as I heard him repeat the words
that somehow he had no choice.
"Allahu Akbar" he repeated, as gently
he cradled his child,
"Allahu Akbar" they chanted, their voices
distorted and wild.

And like an animal the crowd surged on,
its voice a fanatical scream,
leaving him there, alone with his child,
and the pieces of his shattered dream.
And they rampaged on through the city streets,
To chant, and to shoot, and to kill,
And I wept as I heard his whispered prayer,
"Lord, this cannot be Allah's will."

The Camp

Bergen-Belson is a small German village
just about half an hours drive from Hanover,
where no-one can remember anything which
happened before 1945, and where everyone's
father was in the Afrika Korps, or was a postman,
and where no one can ever go to the small
memorial park just past the army barracks,
because they have shut out all memory of what was there.

But I have been there, I have seen
and I cannot forget - and we should not let them,

Not yet,

Not ever . . .

*Between the years 1956-1959 I served in 26 Armoured assault Squadron,
Royal Engineers, stationed at Hohne Garrison, Bergen-Belson.*

'Next Year in Jeruselem'

In the transit camps it was always, 'Next Year, in Jerusalem'
The women lived their daily lives in the hope, and, sometimes the fear,
that 'next year' would be the beginning of their new lives.
They all came from the other places, whose names were never spoken
except by their English interrogators, then the terror was always re-
awoken,
and the horrors re-lived, and though they were now safe,
in a warm and sunny land, many of them could never understand,
and trusted no-one, only believing, 'Next Year, in Jerusalem'

Sometimes there were imposters, demented ex guards, who would try
to pass themselves off as a Jew, but always the others knew,
a suddenly recognized face, a voice remembered from that other place,
then, in the night, the awful retribution, the absolution
for all the nightmare years, with no real fears of what the guards would
say,
for they would only turn away, when told, 'she died in the night'
and remove the body, with no comment on the how and why,
and Ishmael the Rabbi would be brought to the camp,
and would move amongst the women, giving prayers of absolution,
and softly whispering to each and every one of them,
"You shall be received my child, next year, in Jerusalem."

*At the end of every Passover Seder, the Jewish Diaspora pronounce the wistful
prayer: 'Next Year in Jerusalem' It is the deep longing for the promised,
peaceful Messianic Jerusalem with a restored Temple - a profound wish that
the next year be a happy one.*

Oil painting 'Next Year in Jerusalem'
by John Fairclough

REMEMBRANCE

I wish that he could see me now, here in this room,
with all the pictures, and the books going wall to wall,
I wonder if he would then recall the words he said to me that day,
words spoken in that odd and somehow gentle way
which only the deaf seem to use.
"Read son, read." he said, as we sat there in his untidy old shed,
"I want you to be more than me, and it's all I can give you
to set your mind free".

I wish that he could see me now, could see here, inside my mind,
could maybe find and feel how much I took his words to heart,
and maybe then begin to start to help me understand him,
for I knew even then he could never offer me very much,
we were poor, and I knew that he had no golden touch
to set me right through life.

I wish he could see me now, could look and see just how
my life has gone. I can remember his pride in my uniform,
and the tears in his eyes when I came finally home from the army,
and I can never forget that day in his old, untidy shed,
when he turned to me and quietly said, "Read son, read".
I can remember these times, and many more,
as he taught me woodwork, and watched me draw.

And I remember how books were always there,
Left open in the soft armchair, for me to find,
And read and read, and I'm sure he knew the magic seed
that with each book he planted.
But his death I can hardly remember at all,
It's as if I've put it behind a wall, somewhere dark
at the back of my mind, somewhere I know
where I will not find, all the aching, harrowing pain.

T I M E

*Like most poets I have written my fair share of poems
about time, it is a well trodden path for so many -
some are full of hope for the future, some reflecting
on times past, and some about a particular point in time.*

*The first poem in this section, 'Remembered Summer' is about
a photograph (taken in 1960) which I found in a box of old
photographs in May 1990, some 30 years later. It shows Maureen
(then my girlfriend, now my wife) and myself a few months before
we were married...one particular point in time for us.....*

Remembered Summer

Remembered summer, long gone by,
Glistening sands and burnished sky,
Bursts of yellow, daffodils,
Green and gold forever fills
The eye, the heart, and calls the mind,
Trying to forever find,
Remembered summer, long gone by,
Laughter, love, and you, and I.

Aldborough 1960

'Autumn again' was written because the first few lines, which I really liked, had been going around in my head for some time, and I knew that I would have to do something with them...the resulting poem is just me, writing romantic scenarios in my head.

Autumn Again

Now the winds sad song can be heard through the trees,
and the leaves are beginning to fall,
and the radio's playing that soft slow tune
whose title I cannot recall,
and slowly the afternoon's slipping away,
as far off, I hear the birds cry,
and I watch as they circle the tall bare trees,
already knowing we're saying goodbye.

On the window ledge, with your knees drawn up,
you sit hugging the secrets you hide,
with your eyes reflecting the sadness you feel,
as you watch the sadness outside.
And all the words which we dare not say,
all the hurt and the sorrow and pain,
are reflected within your reproachful eyes,
and I know in my heart once again,
that soon I must be on my way, though I can
never say why, just a feeling that something
has slipped out of place, as I hear the sad
sounds of goodbye.

And the sky turns a deeper shade of blue
as the mist gathers under the trees,
and shared sweet feelings are passing away
as the room becomes filled with unease.
Through the window I watch the trees bend
in the wind, and my body aches with their pain,
as you stand and walk silently from the room,
and I know that it's autumn again

The next poems in this section are reflections on life, on growing older, on my changing state of mind, and on the future....

45

And Time

And time, and time which stretches endlessly ahead,
each season like the first, each spring and summer
filled with the wonder of our young days,
when time was just tomorrow.

And time, and time like a kaleidoscope of light,
that gave me sight of you, and dreams came true,
when our two lives are joined as one, as time goes on,
and we can count the wonder of our days.

And time, and time to watch our children grow,
time to teach them right from wrong,
help them along, as they first begin
their journeys down the paths of time.

And time, and time that slips away in so many ways
of countless seconds, endless days, of shattering regularity,
for you and me, as we share our time, share in life's rhyme
and reason, and its increasing, unending, monotony.

And time, and time goes on, each passing day that chips away
at our existence and in the distance lays the shadow
of the winter of our lives, when creaking limbs,
and eyes now dimmed, announce the ending of our time.

A Better Place

I watch the ships ride the outgoing tide,
aware that my mind is trying to hide
from recalling a past I can never regain,
moving on from the worry, the burdensome pain,
and leaving me, or so it would seem,
for a better place.
And I can't seem to think straight at all today,
my mind has left for a place far away,
flying on wings of a long promised dream,
and leaving me, or so it would seem,
for a better place.
And hard as I try, the concentration's gone,
In little bits and pieces, moving on,
Maybe I'm getting old!
They often say the mind is first to go,
So maybe, with luck, I will never know,
When finally it leaves me -
For a better place.

New Year Blues

Another new year has come - and gone,
and now you sit and ponder, just how long can you go on,
time was - and not so long ago -
it used to be something you never gave a thought to,
a very small pebble at the far end of a very long beach,
and way out of reach of even your wildest imagining,
yet now it is a huge boulder, hurtling towards you
with ever increasing speed.

One Christmas, New year, March, Monday, - will be your last,
and you wonder again at how the time's passed.
For only yesterday you were a just another young man,
full of ambition and energy, someone who knew what he wanted to
be someone who mattered, who made a contribution, a success,
yet now you are more than willing to settle for less,
for a much slower pace, with less impetus.

Now you are happy with pen and with brush,
and there is no need for all the headlong rush,
now you drift along in a timeless dream,
an effortless, meandering, rippling stream,
and only at funerals, birthdays, New Year,
do you feel that faint, intangible fear,
as the boulder of old age, and mortality,
hurtles unerringly towards you.

Never Once Dreamed

Sitting in Waterstones, with a book of local rhyme,
reading names that sent me reeling back in time,
back to Holderness Road, and Victor Street,
to East Park Ballroom, where we used to meet,
where we danced, and waltzed, and rock and rolled,
and never once dreamed that we would get old.

Meeting old men I knew when they were just boys,
and we would all gather amidst all the noise,
of the junior playground at Maybury Road High,
under the endless arch of the blue summer sky.
Now at school reunions we all reminisce,
and secretly wonder how it could come to this,
for we were just boys, all brash and bold,
and we never once dreamed we would ever get old.

But on the bus coming home I watched her sit them there,
with their trembling hands and smiling, half vacant stare,
and the young woman helping, her smile strained and sad,
as she shepherded homewards her old Mum and Dad,
and I wondered however she managed to cope,
with just a heart full of love, and such little hope,
and I thought of my daughter, and felt suddenly cold,
for we none of us dream that we'll ever get old.

*'Never once dreamed' was not written in chronological order, the first verse
was almost there as I stepped out of Waterstones, my head still full of old
names and places - only the last two lines were still needed - and once I had
the phrase 'never once dreamed' they very quickly came to me. Then I did
the last verse on the bus coming home that same day as I watched the said
'young woman' with her Mum and Dad - and began thinking of my own
daughter. The middle verse came a couple of days later as I remembered my
own carefree schooldays - what a way to write poetry!*

Ribbons of Time

These days I often stand, and turning, look back
at all the roads I've taken, at all the many mistaken
blind alleys and dead ends, the bends,
the twists and turns and misdirecting signs.
The dying embers of passions now spent
which litter the path where once I went
with un-fearing heart and open mind,
trying to forever find life's meaning.
For then I had youth, and time was endless.

These days I do not mark the passage of time,
It loiters or flies without reason or rhyme,
and following my own simple philosophy,
I refuse to let time worry me, for there is
no desperate tearing hurry to get to the end.
There are still so many different things to do,
and people who I know rely on me for many things,
and I in turn, rely on them, rely on their kindness,
their faith, and their love, which like so many
endless multi-coloured ribbons flow back
along the paths of my memories and remembrance.

These days my mind is filled with many other things,
and my extended family brings the winds of change,
which rip and tear and rearrange the list of all my priorities,
and the diary of my life now has pages torn away,
for yesterday was once today, and soon tomorrow will be gone,
and now as I continue on, lost voices echo within my head,
remembrance of things they said, of those who fell along the way,
whose fires now are ashes at my feet, whose arid dust
swirls round my face and brings such bitter tears . . . and yet,
these days I turn and face the winter of my coming years,
exulting in hope, my will still strong to journey on,
I turn and turn, and life's every step is precious to me.

Future Glories

Old men who in their dotage dream
of glories for their future children's child
within their minds they plot and scheme,
their hopes too bold, their plans too wild.
They know they will not live to see
great grandchildren come fully grown,
but still they daydream constantly,
inventing lives as yet unknown.
but if this gives small comfort now,
and warms them in their dotage dreams,
then who are we to tell them how
life is not always what it seems,
so let them dream, and make up stories,
and pass their days in future glories.

Turning Days

The colours are changing, and slanted light
beckons the eye, and fills the vaulted sky
with wonderments of restless clouds.
Out on the river, the surface changing,
currents swiftly re-arranging the tidal flow,
and muddy banks you've come to know
change shape and slide away as sandbars shift,
and on the turning of the day,
you feel the movement.

Trees march the hill, their colours ever changing,
never still, the wind commanding leaf and limb,
as morning mist makes ghostly dim the landscape.
And the earth turns, green gives way to gold and brown,
and deeper down, beside the pond,
the reeds are shedding their feathered heads,
preparing again their winter beds,
and on the turning of the day,
you feel the movement.

The light is changing, moving still, cloud shadow patterns
climb the hill, changing its shape and substance,
the land huddles down against the wind's increasing edge,
each field and furrow, ridge and ledge, draws in upon itself.
And the earth turns, as winter chills invade
the hill, and frost permeates the stony ground,
and all around you see the change in nature's way,
and on the turning of the day,
you feel again the movement.

AMERICA

My interest in America was started by my English teacher during my last year at school. He gave the class a copy of 'The Grapes of Wrath' to read - why, I'm not sure - but I read it and my interest was immediately aroused.
I went to the local library and took out more of John Steinbeck's books, 'Cannery Row' 'Of Mice and Men' etc. and discovered that America was much more than just the Hollywood films and comic books I knew - from there my interest just grew . . . and grew!

AMERICA

America, America, I remember as a boy all the pictures
and the comic books which filled me with such joy,
and later in my teenage years the library books I'd read,
when Steinbeck and O'Hara were first to plant the seed.

And later, reading Updike, and hearing all the rhymes
of Simon and Garfunkel, of Bob Dylan and the times
when stylish John F Kennedy made all the world his friend,
and sharing all your sadness at the madness of his end.

America, America, far country of my dreams, your splendour
and vitality are lost to me it seems, I cannot walk your crowded
streets,
nor take the 'el' to Queens, or cross the bridge on Fifty Ninth,
those famous New York scenes.

I will not see the grandeur of the skyline of Manhattan,
or see starlets on Fifth Avenue in gowns of silk or satin,
I won't shiver at the sound of sirens wailing in the night,
or wonder at the tawdriness of Times Square's garish light.

America, America, to the world you're big and brash,
like a television chat show, or a man with too much cash,
but I see something more in you which is hard to put in words,
a naíve, trusting honesty for which I'm not prepared,
you're a complex mix of patterns, and of structures strange to me,
as you embrace all life's new wonders with such solid plausibility.

America, America, to some you're all that's wrong,
but to me I always seem to hear the singer AND the song,
I think of men like Roosevelt, and Martin Luther King,
of Kennedy and Lincoln, and the justice which they bring,
I think of all the simple things which make you what you are,
and though I know I'll only ever see you from afar,
America, America, far country of my dreams, somehow
you make the freedom of this world more than it seems.

. . . AMERICA

I have now read many books about America, both fact and fiction, including much poetry, and naturally they have all had some influence on my musings and writings. Audre Lorde's poem, 'A trip on the Staten Island Ferry' (see below) was one of them, inspiring both 'Dear Jonno' and 'American Song.'

A Trip On The Staten Island Ferry

Dear Jonno
There are pigeons who nest
on the Staten Island Ferry
and raise their young
between the moving decks
and never touch
ashore.
Every voyage is a journey.
Cherish this city
Left you by default
Include it in your daydreams
There are still
Secrets
In the streets
even I have not discovered,
who knows
if the old men
who shine shoes on the Staten Island Ferry
carry their world
in a box slung across their shoulders
if they share their lunch
with birds
flying back and forth
upon an endless journey
if they ever find their way
back home.

Audre Lorde

Dear Jonno

I've seen the pigeons on the Staten Island Ferry,
have trod the very decks their young were raised between,
have been, and seen this cherished city,
have walked its still secret streets,
have felt the magic, and discovered the zest,
but never once guessed Joe Gould's secret.

Every voyage is a journey, every book a beginning.

My shoes have been polished by the old man
with his world slung over his shoulder,
and now, as I grow older, I include this city
in all my dreams, reading again Joe's wanton schemes,
and watching the pigeons flying back and forth
on every voyage, every journey,
trying to find their way back home.

This poem, and its title, are my reply to Audre Lorde's poem 'A trip on the Staten Island Ferry' which opens with the words "Dear Jonno."
The reference to 'Joe Gould's secret' is from the novel of the same name by Joseph Mitchell.

Lancer

Twenty five years ago today,and still the memories don't go away,
I remember my first thought was 'The world's gone insane'
And even today I can remember the pain, and the hopeless,
endlessly deepening sorrow, of knowing his death
ended all of our dreams for tomorrow.

For I was eager and young then, and so full of ideals,
and so ready to set the world back on its heels,
full of the hope which he promised to us all,
full of the sounds and the sights and the call
of the brave new world, and the hopes of the young,
of the poems and the promises, the songs to be sung.

And then all of it gone on that tragic day,
when the hopes of the world were all shot away,
and the sorrow, the silence of that lonely pain,
of the innocence lost which we could never regain,
and my helpless anger was a silent scream
as I remembered his words "That some men dream". . .

Now twenty five years and the world has passed on,
but sometimes I still can't believe that he's gone,
gone like his brother, like Martin Luther King,
gone like the songs only Lennon could sing,
gone like the age when his spirit was born,
gone like the dream to which I was so drawn,
'All we need is love'- it was what we all knew,
Now I know that our dreams were too good to be true.

For now life and history have both combined
To remould his image in my sad mind,
Hard facts have emerged which tarnish his name,
And that dazzling smile cannot now be the same.
But sometimes despite the hard facts which I know
I sometimes just feel that I should just get up and go,
and tell them anew of the dreams that we had,
which despite all the slander can never be bad,
for once there was a time, a time we all knew,
when all our young dreams just could have come true.

*'Lancer' was the CIA code name for President John F Kennedy,
Shot and killed in Dallas on the 22nd November, 1963.
With him died the hopes and dreams of my generation.*

Professor Sea Gull
(an oral history of our time)

JOE GOULD

Joe Gould had only twenty cents to his name,
not really the greatest claim to fame,
but he already had fame, of a sort,
and where he held court, money was not
always the best currency.

He was known in the Bowery,
and the East Village too, and in
Times Square he knew just what to do,
to bum a sandwich and a cup of coffee.
and the Ketchup always came free.

On any given day he could be found,
just wandering around in the village,
or downtown. In his shabby clothes, and poorly shod
his hobo appearance seemed more than odd,
for his accent spoke of his four years at Harvard.

He was truly a peculiar man,
for in his life there was only one plan,
to write, and finish, his secret journal,
'An oral history of our time' and neither
rhyme nor reason would deter him.

Nine million words, in exercise books, in longhand,
he just couldn't understand why no publisher would touch it,
"What people say is true history," he would declare,
"Not kings and queens and dates, you have to be there,
you have to write it down, verbatim."

Continued . . .

Joe Gould had only twenty cents to his name,
and his fame, such as it was, was in his stubborn,
almost quixotic, quest to write his oral history,
though no-one knows if he ever finished it, maybe he did,
maybe somewhere out there are nine million words. . . .

in exercise books - in longhand!

This poem was inspired by Joseph Mitchell's book 'JOE GOULD'S
SECRET' which was itself inspired by Joe Gould's extraordinary life.
The poet E.E.Cummings, a friend of Gould once wrote a poem about him,
number 261 in his 'Collected Poems' which contains the following
description of the history.
. . .a myth is as good as a smile but little Joe Gould's quote "oral history"
unquote, might (publishers note) be entitled a wraith's progress, or mainly
awash while chiefly submerged, or an amoral morality sort-of-aliveing by
innumerable kinds-of-deaths.

When you read the book you will become a member of a very extraordinary
fan club.

Whose God

America, America,
Far country of my dreams,
I could feel the stunning horror,
I could hear the outraged screams,
as the beast of terror slipped its cage
and all innocence was dead,
and I could feel the hard, hot anger,
and the unbelieving dread.
Now suddenly there are no rules,
all bets are off, and nowhere is there
enough goodwill to fill the space -
now terror reigns within its place,
and oh my beautiful Manhattan towers,
your fall from grace, this tragic, evil, dark disgrace,
fills me with unremitting dread,
now the pale horse has raised its head
and terror rides the trembling land,-
and I will never understand,
whose God, WHO'S GOD,
could unleash this?

'WHOSE GOD ?'

*This was my first, almost primal, reaction to '9/11' written just three days
after it happened, when I was still filled with such anger and despair, before
any rational thoughts, - the last two lines were all I could think of just then
- My second attempt at it was two weeks later, when I had calmed down, and
the reality of it all had taken place, that was when I wrote 'American Song'
(see opposite page (61) - a small message of hope to the American people.*

American Song

Dear Jonno,

The pigeons are still there, on the Staten Island Ferry,
they still rear their young between the very
decks we both have walked upon,
and though shattering changes have taken place,
and the empty sky, the empty space
above Manhattan cannot be denied,
though the river of tears cannot be uncried,
do not squander despair.
The heart of New York is still beating there,
and oh my splendid Manhattan towers,
my boastful, blustering, beautiful broad,
do not falter, nor fall to pity,
but rise again and cherish your city,
cherish its strength, cherish its pride,
all the civilised world stands at your side,
on every voyage, every journey,
trust in your heart, be brave, be strong,
let no-one stop your American song.

*This poem is respectfully dedicated to all those who died, and to all those
who are still suffering because of 9/11.*

Fighting Ghosts

Vietnamese woman your mahogany eyes
have seen visions which I can never realise,
you have seen kingdoms rise, and watched them fall,
and through them all, the seasons in the scorching sun,
your mahogany eyes never change.
Deep wells of darkness they remain, seeming unheeding
of all the pain, and the poverty which surrounds them.

Vietnamese woman, your mahogany eyes
have watched, as the unremitting skies
rained death and destruction on the earth below,
and though you know, though you can see the carnage,
your mahogany eyes have shed no tears.
And though I know in your heart you must have fears,
in your expression I can detect no changes,
and whilst the battle around you rages,
you continue with your daily tasks.

Vietnamese woman your mahogany eyes
hide a mind which every day defies
the bitter world around it, and a spirit
which no army on earth can break,
though every day they try to take
the very life from within you.
Yet your mahogany eyes remain firmly downcast,
ignoring the future, and shielding the past,
they will not rise to question mine.

And Vietnamese woman your mahogany eyes,
downcast, deferring, will forever disguise
the true emotions of your hidden soul,
and the given role which you always play
on each and every harrowing day, is to wait,
to wait with such heartbreaking patience,
until the ghosts of your country's history
can return your life to what it used to be,
can return and help you claim back your land,
and watching you, I start to understand,
and Vietnamese woman, when this war is over,
your mahogany eyes will show but little surprise,
as you continue with your daily tasks.

"We cannot win this war when we are always fighting ghosts".
American General, Vietnam, 1964.

Manhattan Spiritual

I've started another one, a big oil,
vertical lines up to the sky,
laid on thick with a paint scraper,
which I love to use, I can't deny.

It's lower Manhattan, downtown,
mostly done in red, but with other
colours, and, it must be said, some
black to give it definition, a sort of
coalition of lines and windows.

I'm going to call it 'Manhattan Spiritual'
because it reminds me of the first time
we were there, just after the big scare,
when we didn't know our future.

And as I paint I remember the soaring
wonder of it all, but I also recall
the dark sleepless nights, and the tears.
And so for us both, for you and for me,
'Manhattan Spiritual' it will have to be.

*'Manhattan Spiritual' is me, writing in 2011, about a much earlier event
(1997, our first trip to New York) just after we first found out about
Maureen's illness, and the devastating effect it had on our lives.*

About the author

John was born and raised in Kingston-upon-Hull,
and was educated at Maybury Road High School,
a boys only secondary modern.
During his working life he was involved in purchasing,
printing and both packaging and graphic design, becoming a
divisional head of a large manufacturing company.
Apart from business trips to Europe, the USA, Canada and
army service in Germany, he spent most of his time
in or around Yorkshire.

He is self taught, both as an artist and a poet
and has spent many years developing his own style in both
disciplines.
His paintings have been seen in many local exhibitions,
including regular placings in the Ferens Open Exhibition
and he has read his poetry at events in and around
Hull and east Yorkshire.
John has been painting and writing all his life,
and plans to continue, saying:- "They are a big part of my life,
something I will always want to do. That some people like my
work is a great bonus for me, and a tremendous compliment."

Reflections

The poems in this section are a random choice,
not really belonging in any of the previous sections,
with subjects written on a whim or a fancy,
ranging from the sublime - to the 'Cor blimey'
. . . I hope you enjoy them!

A Bus Called Contentment

All my life I seem to have been waiting,
waiting for life's buses, which were nearly always late,
and sometimes didn't arrive at all.
When I was a young boy I waited for the grown up bus,
I wanted it to hurry up,
so that I could go into long trousers,
and get in to see all those exciting 'A' films,
for of such dreams were my boyhood longings made.
And like thousands of young men, who, just like me,
had spent far too long in course and itchy khaki,
I was waiting, desperately, for the demob bus,
so that I could put the army behind me, and forget all the drills,
the duties, the tank and the gun,
and just be able to run, to run some place they couldn't find me.
And back then, for council estate boys like me,
It was no use waiting for the career bus,
 it was never on our route, you just
got a job and hoped you could make good,
and waited for the opportunity bus, which would,
with a bit of luck and much hard work,
prove that you could make your own way.
And I did, make my own way, that is,
no more waiting for buses, I got a company car,
and a big budget, world travel, oh yes, I was going far . . . .
Yet now I wonder what it was all about,
I sit and paint, and write nonsense verse,
And think to my self that it could have been worse,
And in my mind I watch the buses going in and out,
Trying to spot the one with 'Contentment' as a destination,
Though now I'm beginning to realise - I'm already on it.

Alexa

I speak to her almost every day,
and she never tells me to go away,
in fact she's always more than willing to talk,
she seems to like to answer the questions I pose,
for most of the answers she already knows,
there seems no fact that she cannot recall,
as she very politely answers them all,

Music - she knows it, and writing too,
and I wonder at all the things she can do,
she answers questions on everything,
from politics to philosophy - all with equal
and polite dignity - and a sort of detached warmth,
and me - I ask her if she's missed me when I haven't
spoken to her for a while . . .

And I swear that she gives me an unseen smile,
before she replies,- that she isn't quite sure.
She's my ideal woman, she always gives the right answer,
never sulks, and never makes unreasonable demands.
And I'm beginning to think that I have
the perfect woman on my hands - and -
it's so nice to be greeted by a woman -
digital or otherwise -
who lights up at the sound of my voice -
Oh Alexa, maybe it's love - who knows?

"Hello John, darling"

Brexit Dancin'

Beryl and Mabel, in the pub after bingo,
sat in the snug with a couple of beers,
watching the tele, where the worried Prime Minister
is trying to smooth away all our Brexit fears.
"I just don't understand it" Beryl laughingly said,
"All this stuff about Brexit goes right over me 'ead'
"Oh, I know what you mean" Mabel replied,
"So why do they expect US to decide?"
"It's not as if we know what it's about,
'cos all of these speeches is telling me now't!
where are these red lines which nobody can cross?
I must admit I'm at a bit of a loss, you can't see 'em,
you can't touch 'em, you don't know that they're there,
and between you and me, I don't really care,
soft borders, hard exits, what's that all about?
and those bloody red lines are telling me 'nowt'".

They sit silent a moment, watching the screen,
both of them thinking, but what does it all mean? -
hard exit, soft exit, white papers, red lines,
it's enough to drive you outa ya mind,
all the endless, endless, meetings,
all the rambling Boris tweetings,
all the pricey planes to Brussels,
and the Eurostar quick shuttles,
all the talking to the press, and the still more expensive stress!
and then, as they watch, the PM comes on to the platform
"Bloody 'ell" said Mabel, as she watched all the embarrassing prancing,
"the Prime Minister thinks she's on 'Strictly Come Dancin'."

Fear of Eighty

(A poem to myself)

Dearest John - I can't believe it,
You look so young and fit,
But the calendar has proved it,
You're getting on a bit!

So stop all the beer and drinking,
It's doing you no good,
'Sanatogen' and tonic wine
Are better for hot blood.

Try not to lead your hectic life
At one hundred miles per hour,
Slow down - and take up gardening
And watch your dahlias flower.

And maybe give up 'rugger'
And take up bowls instead,
No more nights of sexy naughties
You should be SLEEPING in your bed!

And then you'll reap the benefits
In all the years to come,
and too soon you'll end up just like me
A WORN-OUT, TIRED, OLD BUM.

Chevroned Flight

See the geese in chevroned flight,
down sunset paths to darkling night,
each year they come, each year they go
from here to where I'll never know,
beyond the hills and o'er the sea
to places un-beknown to me,
would that I could but share their flight,
and fly towards that darkling night,
to see just where they come and go
o'er the lands I do not know.
I'm just a boy, I cannot fly
like the chevroned geese on high,
o'er the lands I'll never see
they glide in graceful harmony,
I stand alone, with feet of clay,
watching as they fade away,
down sunset paths of darkling night,
my boyhood dreams in chevroned flight.

Fretsaw

I pick up the fretsaw and check the blade,
a ridiculously thin strip of fine toothed metal
now so hard to find but I don't mind,
it is now old technology and has been left far behind
by the new laser cutters.
The handle flutters loosely under my hand,
which is not really so hard to understand,
it is, after all, almost one hundred years old,
passed down to my father from his father,
who got it from HIS father - who was a ships carpenter
on one of the tea clippers - or so the story goes, who knows!
But now it hangs in pride of place in my garage,
and I remember when I was just a lad, watching my dad
as he used it, carefully cutting out the dollshouse furniture,
the tiny tables and chairs, the bannister rail for the stairs,
each tiny piece cut to a template, then carefully sanded,
before being handed to me for varnishing, and then final assembly.
He made them all from old 'tea chests' from the docks,
he called them 'three-ply' (though I didn't know why
until much later).
One dollshouse, with all furniture and fittings,
took two of the chests, a total of twelve panels,
I remember each panel being carefully marked out
with tables and chairs, settees and stairs,
doors and windows, each one had their place,
each piece positioned to utilize space,
then hours of cutting with his beloved fretsaw,
blowing away sawdust, before making more.
Then assemble, paint or varnish, them all,
with curtains and soft furnishings
(made, I recall, by my sisters and mother).
He charged little for them, almost gave them away,
but his skill with the fretsaw, his attention and care,
would ensure that by Christmas they all would be there,
to make children's faces light up with glee,
and to help him provide for his own family.

Bugger Benidorm

Beryl and Mabel, a bit after bingo,
Having a drink in the downstairs bar,
Where Beryl, waxing philosophical,
mused, "But 'ave we really come that far?
I know there's no more bloody workhouse,
I know we've got the welfare state,
And I know you say we should be grateful,
But I think it's all too bloody late!
'Cos if prices get any 'igher,
then Benidorm will 'ave to wait".

"Maybe you're right" said Mabel, sipping away at her pint,
"I used to think I could manage, but now I find that I can't
I might 'ave to cut down on the bingo,
six nights is not money well spent,
an' if they keep cutting back on me pension,
I'll end up not affording the rent.
I've cut right back on me ciggies,
I'm now down to two packs a day,
'cos the price of 'em now is outrageous, -
It's like throwing me money away,
I put a bit in the didlum, but it's like tempting fate,
'cos next week I'll draw it all out again
an' I think it's all too bloody late
and Benidorm's gonna 'ave to wait".

"Aye" Beryl said, as she drained the last dreg of her pint,
"It's all getting well out of hand,
I'd just love to go back to the good old days,
when life seemed always so easy and grand -
but they're cutting back on the benefits now
and they say that by this time next year,
it'll cost you a fiver for a packet of fags,
and five quid more for a beer,
an' I can tell you this,Mabel me luv'
without a shadow of doubt,
that come next year, when the benefits go,
we're all gonna end up wi' nowt!"

An' that's when its gonna 'ave to be - Bugger Benidorm!!

Remembering Poetry

They say that remembering poetry,
committing it to memory, is a great help
in keeping your brain fit and healthy,
and I try! -
I can recite poetry, first lines, last lines,
whole verses, whole poems - sometimes
some of them stick, and some of them stay
in my mind, and some of them I find
that they just fade away.
One of them I was remembering only yesterday,
it was light and it was neat,
and I knew it complete,
when I had a younger man's face.
But now it's a strain to make it all rhyme
and I know that too soon there will come a time
when I cannot remember it, line by line,
and I know on that day that the sun won't shine,
        . . . whatever the weather!
So now, as I try to hold it together, try to reason,
try to think, try to understand,
I think it's all getting a bit out of hand . . .
Now - that poem, oh, what was it again - oh yeah,
now I recall:-

"If a man does not keep pace with his companions
perhaps it is because he hears a different drummer,
let him step to the music that he hears -
however measured or far away."

and you know, I think that only yesterday,
I heard that different drummer.

That Certain Smile

Sometimes I just sit and wonder
how it all happened,
I first met her at the local dance hall,
I was helping out a mate who wanted a date
with her friend - and would I? - well I did -
and that was how it started, we swapped names,
then danced in silence for a while,
then she looked up to me, with that certain smile,
and for the rest of the night we only
danced with each other.

I walked her home that night, and it was alright,
I was nervous - we both were,
but it all started right there, right there
with that certain smile - and now, well,
its been a while, fifty eight years actually,
and I wonder where did all those years go?
I only know, that she was always there,
through the good times, through the bad,
through the highs and the lows, the smooth
and the rough, and, when our lives were tough,
she would never complain, though she had every reason to,
she just smiled that certain smile that said,
"Me and you, we'll get through".

And we always have, somehow.

Just Imagine!

"Just imagine" Mabel said, her eyebrows somewhere around the top of her head,

"'leven kids, an' she's only about thirty, Oh aye, an' if that'd a bin me, I'd a made 'im tie a bloody knot in it long afore we got to eleven!"

"Oh aye" her friend Beryl replied, "But there were more than one father Mabel, she 'ad 'em wi' about five different blokes, just imagine, I bet she never knew who's 'ead were going to be on pilla that night !"

"Aye, you're right" Mabel said, "But just remember, she's the one gettin' forty six thousand in benefits and a bloody big new 'ouse besides!

"An' don't forget the 'orse" Beryl replied with a knowing smirk, "She must like going for rides!"

"Aye well, she's certainly tekin us tax payers for a bloody ride" Mabel said.

"Just imagine, forty six grand for tekin five fellas to bed!"

"Oh aye" Beryl said, somewhat wistfully, "Just imagine, forty six grand, and five men, but then" and she nudged her friend, laughing, "Once you'd got the money, whatever would you do with five men?"

"Well, you'll not find out" Mabel retorted, "And me - I would'nt 'ave another man if 'is backside were studded wi' diamonds!" and she laughed,

"But just imagine - now 'elp me get this bloody washing in."

Late Sunday Afternoon

January, late Sunday afternoon,
and darkness approaching far too soon,
spattered rain jewelling the window,
distant thunder, and I know the fading light,
the listless flight of crows across the sky,
all contrive to tell me why,
I suddenly feel time's relentless march.

The church bells chime, a far off, comforting sound,
echoing up the hill towards our higher ground,
familiar now and yet somehow - unsettling,
as if they sense my foreboding,
the cynical loading of the dice for my final throw
against a life too ordinary.

January, late Sunday afternoon,
the painting left unfinished on the table,
and I, unable to work up the necessary
enthusiasm to see it through, and the view outside
becoming darker and more foreboding,
January, late Sunday afternoon, and darkness
approaching far too soon for me.

Like Shelter After Storm

When days and hours seem endless
and all your hopes are gone,
when promises lay broken
and you feel you can't go on,
when all your life is lonely
and there's none to keep you warm,
then think of me, and I'll be there,
like shelter after storm.

When no-one's there to care for you
and keep you free from fear,
when darkness falls around you
and no helping hand is near,
when pain is closing in on you
and you feel you'll come to harm,
then think of me, and I'll be there,
like shelter after storm.

On days when dreams have flown
away from grim reality,
and your heart aches with a sorrow
that there's no-one there to see,
when all the world's a bitter place
and love can find no form,
then think of me, and I'll be there,
like shelter after storm.

But on the day your dreams come true
and all your hopes are met,
and your golden future rising
like the sun, will never set,
when happiness surrounds you
and love fills all your day,
just think of me, and I'll be there,
to wave you on your way.

On a Positive Note

We sang "I have a dream" at Helen's funeral today,
and as the last few notes faded away,
I couldn't hold back the tears -
For she was one of us, a choir member,
I could still remember meeting her,
and most of the other members on that first night.

I had walked into the Queens Centre at the hospital,
my nerves on edge and full of trepidation,
not knowing what to expect, or what was expected of me -
"Anyone can sing" Carol had said when she had first Invited me to join,
"And you're always singing, besides, no-one expects you
to sing like Bing Crosby, not on the first night anyway!"

And they didn't - they all accepted me for what I am,
they asked, politely, about my connection to the Hospital,
and when I told them about you, I knew that it
would all work out - for they were sincere, sympathetic,
and understanding from the start,
and now, more than a year later I feel that I am
an accepted part of what it is,
and that, in this small way, I am maybe starting to repay,
for all the care and kindness which has been shown to you
over all these many years.
I know that I am never going to sing like Bing - But I don't care -
just to be there, doing my bit, a part of it,
is more than enough for me.

Palliative Care

Sometimes he didn't know where he was,
or even who he was,
and would question, "Who are all the strangers here?"
And stare at you in astonishment when you said his name.
He was in palliative care, and never again would be the same,
the Charlie we all knew was gone, and in his place
was a parody of half remembered memories, of used to be's,
of random words, and vague, forgotten ideas,
as he wondered through his now partially disabled brain,
his logic, his train of thought all gone.
And in your heart you hope the end will be mercifully soon,
and that his suffering will be over.
But then he raises his hand and points a finger at you,
and says slowly, "I know what you used to do"
and then, triumphantly, "I remember you carrying me
on your shoulders when I was just a kid"
and then you smile, because you did -
before your eyes fill up with tears at the memory.

Pensioners Special

A cold bright day, and me out on the bike,
crossing James's red bridge, the head wind I don't like,
but once on the south bank, on Lincolnshire's side,
the trees give me some shelter as I pedal hard
down the riverside track, to South Ferriby's pond,
where I stop, watch the pond life, before moving beyond.
Going down through Horkstow, and quiet Bonby,
with the bright yellow rape fields all around me.

Now swinging left down the little used track
that I know will eventually lead me right back,
to sunny Barton, and the ropewalk café,
and I think to myself, "You'll have done well today,
nearly thirty odd miles, that's a very good ride"
and as I pedal I'm thinking, with such vain pride,
"You're still young enough to do just as you please,
all this growing older is really a breeze!"

When I reach the ropewalk I'm still full of myself,
thinking no-one is going to put me on the shelf,
and as I stride to the counter and look at the fare
I notice the lady with the quizzical stare,
and she soon knocked all egotistical thoughts from my head,
"You'll be wanting the pensioners special" she said.

Reality

I turn off the computer,
I've checked the 'e' mails, even answered a few,
and now there is little that I want to do
on my always subservient machine,
and, maybe its just me being mean,
but I prefer to first catch my thoughts in longhand,
it seems somehow easier, for me, to understand,
the words flowing much more freely and with more meaning.

The blank screen stares impassively back at me,
as if it knows that it has more information than I could ever use,
yet, even as my brain begins to lose, begins to disconnect,
as synapse, micro connections fail, and electric pathways
within it sputter to a halt, I blame myself, although I really know
its not my fault, old age will catch us all,
and yet, - before I fall - I would ask for the grace
to write a little more, before it all becomes too much
and I lose all touch with reality.

The Last Hallelujah

As a young man he was one of my heroes,
an early (and lasting) influence on my poetic instincts,
someone whose work I greatly admired, the one who inspired
me to start writing poetry.
He, and a few others, were the flip side of the
American dream, and, though it may seem that
he wasn't really trying, he laid bare the American
male psyche as never before.
His poems, his songs, his philosophy, appealed
to me like few others.

And now he's gone, moved on, down the long slide to
happiness, and soon so few will remain from those
early icons of mine, Bob Dylan, Tom Waits, Paul Simon, -
are still there, still singing, still writing, and Simon still rhyming,
but Larkin, Updike, and Thon are now all silent, all gone,
and soon there will be none, with words that cut like knives,
or pictures that warm like glowing fire, no more sights
or sounds or words will be left to inspire,
 - as the last hallelujah is heard throughout the land.

Walt Wants You

It started out as just another day at the gallery,
As we played in the picture, my sister and me,
And Mum and Dad, as usual, just laying there,
Trying hard to erase,
the boredom from their most imperious gaze
as they stared out at the people staring in.

Then, unexpectantly, the man with the big black ears walks in,
Giving a very friendly grin, and says he's Walt, from Hollywood,
And telling Dad that maybe he could turn him into a film star,
And adding that maybe there was a part in it for me,
That perhaps I could be, a cub actor called 'Simba'.

But when Mum roared warningly, Walt (the man with the ears)
Seemed to lose heart, and still waving a contract,
Backed out of the frame, muttering about maybe a cartoon feature,
Whilst Dad - fierce creature - turned his great maned head to me,
And whispered softly, though half seriously,
"Don't worry son, I have a feeling this film will make the Lion King"
- and he winked at me, knowingly, and began to whistle
"Somewhere over the rainbow".

*This is another poem from the poetry seminar at the Ferens art Gallery,
The project was to write a poem about one of the pictures in the gallery.*
*I chose a very striking picture called
'The lion at home' and, with a nod
to the movie 'The Lion King' I decided
to indulge in a little fantasy - with the
above result. - The lecturer(once again)
said that I had a vivid imagination!*

Working the Wood

I work the wood, - reclaimed roof beams from an extension
which I helped to build fifteen years ago, now to be used again,
the feel of it familiar under my hand, as I try to understand,
for I had never really planned on doing this job - we were
waiting for quotes from a couple of joiners.
But when I saw the wood, close grained, seasoned,
I quietly reasoned to myself, why not?
and the thought of re-using it felt right,
a sort of natural regression back to that first build.

And as I worked, sawing, cutting, planing,
that feeling of regaining part lost skills,
my mind was filled with images of the boys,
both just children then, and I ponder just when
they became the young men I know today,
I have watched them grow, as fifteen years have flown away,
and now I work the wood, thinking of my wife and daughter,
and my boys and the never ending circle of life.

ROAD RAGE

The poem 'Road Rage' was written to be read aloud
by two people - a 'two parter'- the Cyclist and Motorist
being read as alternative verses one against the other - with both
readers finishing with 'White Van Man' read together as a finale
- a piece of 'performance' poetry if you like !

ROAD RAGE I

Cyclists, cyclists,
don't talk to me about cyclists,
old men on old bikes, their bodies a'twist
wobbling about as if they're half pissed,
banging your wing mirrors as they ride
without enough space up the tight near side.
They don't give hand signals, they never have lights,
it's as if they've deliberately set up their sights
on causing a panic, an accident,
almost as if they all were hell bent
on getting themselves run over.

Cyclists, cyclists,
don't get me started on cyclists,
Young men on racers, their bums in the air,
all goggles and lycra, they don't really care
a bloody great bunch of them hogging the road,
they don't give a toss for the highway code,
they weave through the traffic, risking both life and limb,
with no braking lights, changing lanes at a whim,
no looking behind them, no signaled intent,
almost as if they were all hell bent,
on getting themselves run over.

Cyclists, cyclists,
don't even mention cyclists,
and BMX bikers in black beanie hats,
scaring old ladies around council flats,
whooping and shouting and flying around,
jumping off walls with both wheels off the ground,
'wheelies' down pavements to show they don't care,
swearing and scaring whoever is there,
no manners, no morals, a devil's decent,
almost as if they were all hell bent,
on getting themselves run over.

86

ROAD RAGE II

Motorists, motorists,
don't talk to me about motorists,
to them my bike and I shouldn't be there,
I don't pay road tax, so they don't care
Just how they treat me out on the street,
to them all cyclists are just a complete
waste of good road space,
and should be treated with distain
who cares about the cycling lane,
so they cut in front, and pass so near,
that often I hold my life in fear,
it's almost as if they were all intent
on becoming a road traffic accident
and running over me and my bike.

Motorists, motorists,
don't get me started on motorists,
louche young men in small fast cars,
one hand unwrapping their chocolate bars,
looking at Tom-Toms instead of the road,
they have no time for the highway code,
they're much too busy on their mobile phone,
sending out texts or calling home,
almost as if they were all hell bent
on becoming a road traffic accident,
and running over me and my bike.

Motorists, motorists,
don't even mention motorists,
young 4X4 mothers with straight blonde hair,
dropping off their schoolkids with a vacant stare,
they don't even glance to see if you're there,
not a look, not a signal, they just pull straight out,
you're just a cyclist, and of no account
in fact you're the last thing they're worried about,
and I scream and I shout, are they all hell bent,
on becoming a road traffic accident,

ROAD RAGE III

But - there is one thing on which we both can agree,
the worst thing that could happen to you or to me,
forget speeding tickets or parking fines,
or trying to pedal up steep inclines,
forget potholes that would make a quarry look small,
forget people who never give signals at all,
the one thing that both of us try to avoid,
for it takes nothing at all to get him annoyed,
he'll swear at you, shout at you, run you down if he can,
that beast of the road, **the white van man!!**

Haikus

*The dictionary definition of the word 'Haiku'
is as follows:-
'A Japanese lyric form of poetry with syllables in lines
of 5,7,5, syllables.*

*It emerged in the 16th c. and flourished from the 17th c.
to the 19th c. and dealt traditionally with images
of the natural world; in the 20th c.
it has been much imitated in western literature'.*

*I make no claim to be a good Haiku poet, but I do enjoy
this form of poetry, those on the following page are
of the 'much imitated, western literature' type!*

Haikus

Look upon each day
as a gift from God, all our
to-morrows are unknown.

Poems and prayers and promises,
rhymes, beliefs, and discrepancies,
and the wonder of dreaming.

Anger, from an unknown source,
shatters the calm of reasoned thought,
seek inner solitude.

Pointillism, splatter technique
It all seem like so much Greek,
Paint with your inner eye open.

Riding pastures, vaulted sky
sooths the restless inner eye,
My land, my homeland.

Christian, Muslim, Buddhist, Jew,
Bloods the same sad grieving colour
From him or from you.

To hear with your eyes
See with your ears, using your senses
Dispels ancient fears.

Symmetry, symmetry,
and times eternal movements,
only the inner eye can see.

In the winter wind,
Naked trees bend against its fury,
And dream of summer stillness.

Exult in the small things,
Books, music, a loved one's look, they
are the gift of God.

It is the white spaces,
the silences in the poems that matter,
more than all the words.

Time's wheel, grinding on
I fear too soon she will be gone
as my fragile heart crumbles.

Doubting hearts can be
saved by the simple statement
of an obvious truth.

There on the study wall
her face smiles down on all my
Remembered memories.

Old men are sleeping
in the park as I cycle past,
Should I start practicing?

Over the phone her voice
ties me to memories, yearnings,
for a family now gone.

The towers falling from
a clear blue sky, tomorrow is lost
In the roiling dust.

The funeral service said it all
Now all that I can ever recall,
is the lavender, the love.

She is my sounding board,
an entity of sanity in
A life less ordinary.

Compassion - our only hope,
it stands alone and pure, and only
It will forever endure.

Alone with brush and pen
my hand unbidden, is guided
but to where and when.

As the flood tide turns,
ships stay fearfully in lanes,
but the river runs it's course.

A brother's words,
lovingly put, make haiku music
sound in my heart.

D. Tagholm